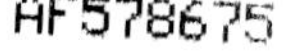

Table Of Contents

<u>The First Christmas</u>

Once there was a small community in the mountains. They were friendly, but hardworking. None of the families had children.

They decorate the village every winter with Christmas lights. In each house, there was a Christmas tree and stockings that were hung over the fireplace.

Ginger biscuits were delicious and the candle light lit the night.

Everyone hoped that Santa would bring gifts to their stockings in the morning, but they found them empty every time. They were not aware that Santa never stops at their homes.

A wooden carriage pulled up to the village bakery one day. A

A poorly dressed man entered the bakery to ask for bread for his little girl. He was extremely poor and had no money to buy food. According to the baker:

"If you are looking for work, you might stay here and be my assistant. Your wife could bake the pastries and biscuits.

The family of the poor was delighted to hear that and continued to live in the small village.

The days were flying by and winter came back.

All Christmas lights were on and the houses were beautifully decorated.

The snow started falling in large flakes. Within a few hours, everything was covered in a fluffy white blanket.

The stockings, which were hung like ever over the fireplace the next morning, were filled with gifts.

People understood why Santa was stopping there for the first time. It was because it was the first time Santa had stopped in the village. And where children live, everything is pure and magical. Santa will remember the tiny village lit up with sparkling Christmas lights and will stop there from now on.

The Legend Of Christmas Stockings

A nobleman was very kind and his wife died from an illness. He left behind three beautiful daughters, including the poor nobleman.

The nobleman eventually lost all his wealth and the family moved into a cottage owned by a peasant. There, the three daughters took care of their cleaning, sewing, and cooking.

The father was even more unhappy when it came to the daughters getting married. A daughter couldn't marry without having dowries, money, and property.

The girls washed and dried their clothes one evening.

It was Christmas Eve night, and Saint Nicholas saw that the whole family had gone to bed. He then passed the nobleman's house and took three bags of gold out of his pouch. They fell into the stockings of the girl, and he threw them.

When they woke up in the morning, the three young girls had enough gold to marry and were happily dancing around their father. That was a miracle and the nobleman didn't worry again. Believe in your dreams, and they will come true.

Every child in the world has since then hung stockings above the fireplace to wait for Saint Nicholas with his beautiful gifts.

The Magical Christmas Letter

Raphael was a small boy once. He heard the children from the nearby neighborhood who were writing Santa Claus letters.

He began to laugh, saying:
"I believe Santa brings gifts to all children, so there is no need to write a letter."
Another child replied, "It's not true. Santa sent his elf to read our letters. If they make the gift in the workshop, it's possible."
Raphael returned home, and decided to write Santa a long letter. He was a spoilt little boy and thought he would get all he wanted. He had the idea to ask Santa for hundreds upon hundreds of toys, as well as dozens of sweets and biscuits.
He asked his mother to give him a piece of paper, and a pen. He sat down and began to write.
His mother bought him a new pen.
Raphael began to write again, but all of his words disappeared immediately.
He tried to change the pen again, but it was the same, so he called his mother.
"Mom, may you come here to a second?"
His mom saw the situation and immediately understood it. "My dear, Santa's letter must be magical.
Believe what you write, or else Santa won't be able to read it. Faith is the only thing that will keep your words from disappearing forever.
Raphael was stunned at his mother's reaction and gave up. The next morning, Raphael woke up to see all the Christmas presents. He ran to open all the beautifully wrapped boxes, but he soon realized that none of them were for him.
All of them had tags with their names on them, but he couldn’t find his name anywhere.
He understood Santa exists, he was able to be thankful for his gifts and believed in the magic of Christmas.
To apologize for his behavior, he wrote Santa a letter.

When Santa Got Sick

It was once very cold. All was covered in snow, and it was freezing all day. Nobody was there because the roads and ground were covered in snow.

People were excited about Christmas and wondering when Santa would arrive. He couldn't fly on his sleigh.

Santa's Town was no different. All the elves worked hard to complete all the presents on time. The reindeers were hiding out, as they would become ice statues outside.

Santa was lying in bed, wrapped in a thick blanket, and coughed and sneezed.

One elf said, "Santa, you can't transport all gifts, look at how sick you are."
"It's time to change the Christmas date," said one elf.

Santa replied, "To change Christmas?", "I will never miss one Christmas."
"My magical sleigh is able to fly through all kinds of weather."

"Your magical sleigh ...",talked to the elf.

He began to whine, hoping that the sleigh would appear.

"The sleigh seems lost. It might be hidden in the snow, which could explain why it doesn't respond to your whistle.

Santa got up and went to the workshop, where the elves were making toys. He knew that everyone was eagerly awaiting their Christmas gifts so he couldn't miss them, even though he was sick.

How could Santa find his sleigh? He called the Wizard of Ice, his friend, and asked him to give him some magical dust to melt the snow.

The elves brought a large bag to Santa's house. When Santa opened the bag, thousands and thousands of silvery stars began flying across the sky.

The snow began to melt for a few seconds before the reindeers were able to pull the sleigh out. The magical stars suddenly changed into shimmering dust, which fell to the ground and frozen everything.

The little elves filled the sleigh with sweets and toys wrapped in colorful boxes and cleaned it.

Santa began his journey around the world after all the children had gone to bed and nobody was there. Although it was hard work, the reindeers helped Santa.

Be faithful and good, because Santa will always arrive every year.

The Lost Snowflake

Haston, the happy elf, finished his work in Santa's workshop. He went into his bedroom and looked out of the window. Although it was dark, the sky was filled with shimmering stars that glow at night. He was afraid of the cold because he

He will freeze if he goes outside.

A snowflake appeared in his room when he opened the window to get some fresh air. It was delicate and had the perfect shape of a sophisticated, elegant star.

Haston wondered if the flake was interested in being his friend or why it came into his room.

The snowflake said, "I felt the wonderful smell of ginger biscuits. I came into your bedroom."

The little elf replied, "You can stay here and become my friend."

They began to play together and ate ginger biscuits, telling each other funny stories.

The snowflake said, "I would love to see Santa's workshop"

The happy elf brought his friend to the workshop. There were many elves working together to complete the toys in time for Christmas. They all wanted to touch the snowflake, which looked magical and mysterious when they first saw it.

The snowflake began to melt and silvery drops started to drip from his.

Eyes.

Haston realized it was too hot so he opened the windows.

The flake was sent outside.

The snowflake suddenly regained its sparkling shine and flew away.

A few days later, the smiling elf Haston lost his smile after missing his snowflake friend. He decided to conquer his fear of the cold and be strong. He put on his gloves and a hat, and he went outside to search for his friend.

Since then, they have been playing happily together every time it snows.

The Christmas Angel

One day before Christmas Eve, everything was going wrong in Santa's house. Mrs. Claus has destroyed all the ginger biscuits. At the workshop, the elves failed to finish all the toys, and the reindeers lost their sleigh. Santa also didn't find any Christmas trees.

Santa said, "This year everything's a disaster", and he was angry.

The elves worked all night to wrap all the toys in colorful boxes and finish them off.

The reindeers broke up and began digging in the snow for the magical sleigh.

Mrs. Claus made the ginger biscuits again, but she was careful not to burn them.

The next morning, everything was ready. The sleigh had been found, cleaned and filled with all the presents. So that the gifts are delivered correctly, the older elf carefully read the letters of the children.

Mrs Claus wrapped the candy canes and biscuits in silvery boxes.

Santa filled his bag with magical dust to make the sleigh fly faster. The reindeers also put on their golden bells so they can jingle along the way.

Everyone was pleased that they were able to complete the work on schedule.

Santa Claus was born:

"We forgot about the Christmas tree. How can we have Christmas without a Christmas tree?"

It was dark, and they couldn't find any trees.

A shimmering light suddenly appeared in the sky. It seemed to be getting closer and closer and was becoming brighter and more prominent.

It was an angel in white, holding a Christmas tree in his hands.

He placed the tree on the sleigh, and he flew off.

People hang an angel from that night on Christmas trees to express gratitude for the angel who saved Christmas

The Magical Phone Calls

It was winter, with snow falling and wind blowing. The children were all upset that Santa Claus couldn't be reached outside so they couldn’t send their letters. The weather was improving, but they were hopeful.

A few days later, the entire town was covered in snow. People couldn't open their doors and everyone was trapped in their houses.

The children were very worried about Santa getting their letters.

The Spirit Of Christmas lived far away in a castle of glittery blue and ice. When he heard children laugh when they opened their presents, he was happy every year. He saw everyone disappointed this year so he decided to do something.

"If I melt snow, how will Santa arrive with his Sleigh?"

He went to the bookshelf, looking for the Book Of Winter. It contained all the magical information about snow, Christmas, and cold weather.

He began to look into what he could do for the children to send Santa letters.

He read through the night, and finally came up with the right decision. He quickly went to Santa's workshop to ask the elves for hundreds of red phone models.

Within a matter of hours, all the phones had been made. The Spirit Of Christmas visited all homes and placed one small red phone into the children's bedroom. These phones were magic and children were connected to Santa's workshop the next morning when they picked up their handsets. A elf answered, and he wrote all of the wishes for Christmas.

All the presents were completed in a matter of days.

All the presents were delivered by Santa Claus and his reindeers on Christmas Eve.

The Spirit of Christmas looked at the children who had opened their gifts ..... and went to bed until next year, when Christmas will be back.

A Special Christmas Tree

Abette was a large conifer. Many other conifers were also growing, and each year people would bring them home to decorate. They were also always planting new little trees.

Because Abette was so large, he couldn't fit into a house. Abette was always jealous of the friends he had.

He was brought home to be made a Christmas tree. He also wished that he could have lights, angels, and other decorations. He saw only snow and the cold wind of winter.

The people of that small town saw the need for a play area and decided to build one next to the large tree.

They built a wooden house for children to buy sweets. After some time, the place looked like a little fairy town.

They were delighted and wanted to show their gratitude to their parents, so they decorated Abette and made him a massive Christmas tree.

Abette lowered the branches to allow children to hang ornaments, bells, silver tinsel, and angels. Abette was transformed into a beautiful Christmas tree by the addition of shiny lights.

He was so happy that he longed to be adopted by his family. Now he is the Christmas tree for all of the children. He is happy now and the children around him are singing and dancing carols.

The Snowflakes Necklace

Denise was a small girl when she was born. She loved toys and dolls, and each year asked Santa for more. She had an unusual idea this year. She wanted a necklace made from snowflakes.

She found a small, cute box with the tag "For Denise" on Christmas Eve. She opened the box, but there were only a few water drops inside. She began to cry and became upset.

The Snow Fairy visited her and said:

"-The snowflakes necklace must be kept in your heart to keep it from melting.

Denise replied, "Ok, then freeze my heart so that I can wear my beautiful necklace."

A beautiful necklace with blue snowflakes shimmering around her neck was created. She was happy and took a look at herself in the mirror.

After some time, Denise decided that she would go outside and play with the other kids. She was dressed and ran towards them. She was shouting:

"I want to play alongside all of you."

The children looked at her as if she was not there. They didn't answer her second call.

The girl returned home, confused and confused. The Snow Fairy appeared and told her:

"The children have a warm and open heart, but they don't hear you. After you asked for the snowflakes necklace, your heart became cold and frozen."

"-May my friends be back?" Denise said, "I will give up my necklace if it is possible to turn as I was before."

The spoiled little girl realized that friendship was more important than any other thing. She raced to join her friends at the skating ring.

One Greedy Elf

Wanton was an Elf who worked many years in Santa's workshop.

He was just like the rest of them, a little green elf. But he was greedy and gluttonous. He was in the sweets department and, while he was packing sweets, he tasted everything.

He had to make all the candy canes by himself this year. He made the sweets according to the recipe. He ate and ate throughout the night. He realized that he had not made enough sweets when he got up in the morning to get all his gifts ready.

He began to cry, knowing that Santa would be upset. Wanton was one of many children who wanted candy canes. He was desperate and ran around looking for a solution. It was impossible to make hundreds in a few hours.

He went to the Wise Elf, and cried:

"I know that I made a mistake. I ate all of the sweets and don't know what to do. "It's too late to make cookies again."

"Yes, you alone would not make it. But together with all the other Elfs, we can make all the needed candies."

So Wanton began to ask and beg all the Elfs for their help.

"I promise next year that I will also help you, and I will never again make this mistake." Please help me."

Instead of taking a break after all the hard work, the elves went into the kitchen to create beautiful candy canes.

They made hundreds of sweets in less than an hour, so that everything was ready for Santa when he arrived.

Wanton was grateful and happy to have such great friends.

He was always there to help everyone.

The Witch Who Fell In Love

It was one day before Christmas, and the snow continued to fall all night. The roads were icy white, and there were floating frozen flakes in the air. The children were decorating their homes and getting ready for Santa's visit. Meanwhile, the elves and reindeers were busy creating millions of gifts.

They were cleaning out the sleigh. There was no one around, only a witch flying about.

But then, her broom suddenly broke and the witch fell onto a roof.

The moon saw the smile and began to laugh. When she saw the beautiful smile on the face of the moon, the witch fell in love. So she decided to give the moon a gift. She opened her bag and looked inside. There was nothing adorable in the bag. Her ragged bag contained spiders, black roses, and other Halloween-related scary stuff.

She pulled out her magic wand, and spoke a spell that turned everything into sweets. Ginger bread, almond biscuits, and candy canes began to appear from the bag.

The witch said, "This is my gift to you, I will return every year and bring you a gift so that you can always remember I will always remain your friend!"

To the moon, she sent her shining beam to say thank you for the sweets.

Even a witch discovered that Christmas is a time for family and friends, and a time of thanksgiving and joy.

Chocolate Biscuits

Billy was alone at home. He got up and took out a bowl to pour the milk. He opened a cocoa powder sachet and dropped a spoonful into the milk, creating a large.

Brown cloud. The milk was sprayed with cocoa, which formed small islands of brown. He added two eggs and some butter to the mixture and stirred. His ocean was filled with funny-shaped waves. A little brown sugar was added to his sea, creating dark lines.

When he added the flour, it started to snow heavily. It covered the entire area at first, but then large lumps formed when he stirred it with a wooden spoon. He continued stirring and the lumps started to disappear. Then he dived into the white mixture, which turned into a firm dough.

He began to stretch the dough and cut various shapes from biscuits, including stars, hearts, trees, and hearts.

After baking the biscuits for 20 minutes, he added some icing sugar to them. They were beautiful.

He placed them on a silver platter, right in middle of the dinner table.

Everyone was stunned and agreed that Billy's chocolate biscuits tasted amazing.

Delicious.

He was happy, as he thought that it was his Christmas gift.

Parents.

The Koala Family

Kim was a baby Koala who lived in Australia with her family. Father Koala worked all day, while mother Koala rested because she couldn't work as hard due to being pregnant.

They decorated the house and made the Christmas tree. Santa was coming soon. Kim wrote her a letter.

Santa asked Santa for many sweets and toys long ago.

Kim and her mom made cookies and pudding, and placed scented candles around the house to make it look nice for Christmas.

They went to bed together, but mother Koala went into labor during the night and gave birth to a beautiful Koala.

Kim woke up in the morning and immediately went to the Christmas tree to look for her presents. She heard something, it was like someone was crying.

She looked up to see her mother holding her baby Koala.

She hugged her brother and kissed him. She went to open her Christmas gifts, but she didn't play. Then, she looked at her brother and thought that it was the best Christmas present ever.

Christmas is more special when everyone is together.

A Christmas Miracle

Louis was once a poor little boy. Louis' parents couldn't afford sweets and could barely find the money to buy food for him.

He wrote Santa a letter one day and asked for sweets.

Although he didn't have a Christmas tree to decorate, he did find some green branches that he could use and decorated them with colored paper. He was a good boy who listened to and helped others.

Santa saw this and decided to do something for the child. Everyone went to bed on Christmas Eve.

Santa came and brought lots of gifts to the family. He then went into Louis's bedroom and threw some magic dust. There were thousands of shimmering

Little stars began to fly and touch things, turning them into sweets.

The windows turned into almond cakes, and the lamp into a giant lollypop, while the door became a massive chocolate biscuit. His bed became a sponge cake, his pillow gingerbread, and his blanket into soft cotton candy.

Louis believed he was still dreaming when he woke up in the morning. He rubbed his eyes but nothing was there.

He began to taste it all. He heard a voice say:

"Don't you ever forget. Miracles are possible at Christmas.

<u>The Tinsel Dress</u>

Sarah wanted to be a fashion designer as a young girl. Sarah had many interests.

There were many dolls to play with, and she was busy designing formal Christmas dresses.

Some dresses were longer than others, while others were shorter. Others were made of silk and velvet. To make the dresses special, she added glittery beads and other materials.

Her fashion show should conclude with a doll in a bridesmaid dress. It was difficult for her to find white fabric, which was really a problem. She wondered, "How can you make a wedding dress?"

She suddenly had an idea.

She took a sheet of white paper and cut two triangles. She glued the upper portion of the necklace with white pearls to the doll's neck.

She also used silver tinsel she had gathered from the Christmas tree to finish the bottom of her dress.

"I'm sure Mom wouldn't mind,"

It was a beautiful combination of silver, white, and shiny pearls.

Sarah's fashion show concluded with Sarah wearing her special dress, which no doubt won any competition in dresses design.

The Toy Shop

There was a huge window with icicles hanging from it. The door was open and shut continuously. The door opened and closed continuously. An old man entered, smiling at the children. It was the town's new toy shop.

It was hard to describe the movement and noise under the bright lights.

Children laughed and talked to one another.

A train ran on a green table and then hid in dark tunnels.

After that, you can climb on the cardboard-painted mountains.

There were many toys on the shelves: dolls and teddy bears, wooden boat, cars, etc.

Trucks. They seemed all alive.

The seller offered to buy the old man a cute toy.

She found two mice in a box. One was large and one was small. They were wearing blue woolen socks, painted shoes, and whiskers made from white thread. The tale was made of black rubber.

As a Christmas gift to an orphan boy, he only needed one toy. However, the big mouse was grabbing the smaller mouse so he bought them both together.

The orphan child began to weep when he opened his gift. He said:

"I hope that one day I will find someone who will hug me and protect my feelings."

He was overcome with emotion and decided to take the boy home.

They have lived happily ever since and now spend Christmas together.

One Tree Without Lights

Children organized a Christmas Eve concert in front their school.

All their grandparents, parents, and friends were invited. The week was full of rehearsals. They decided to decorate the whole school yard on the last day.

They brought three Christmas trees, and they hung all kinds of stars, tinsels, angels, bells. They switched on the lights at the end.

The lights on two trees were brightly colored, while the lights on the third tree were only white.

He was jealous of his friends and wanted to shine like them. He thought that they sparkle better with bright lights and this is why he was punished by receiving only white lights.

The jealous tree took the lights from his friend, and gave them to him the white ones, just as everyone was falling asleep.

The concert was about set to start. The children were excited and switched on the Christmas lights.

Only two trees had lights. Two white lights and one with colorful lights.

Although the lights were taken by the jealous tree, they did not switch on. He became very mad and realized that he shouldn't be rude and mean to his friends.

Everyone is unique and beautiful in their own ways.

Even with the white lights, he would have been even more shining. He is now listening to the carols, and is embarrassed by his actions.

Helda The Paintbrush

Helda was a painter and made a whole collection of paintings for Daniel, her friend. He was asked to make something for school one day. He immediately thought of a painting.

He realized that he had finished all of the colors when he opened the paint box.

There were only two remaining colors: white and black.

Daniel thought, sadly, "It's impossible paint only with black and white."

Helda, the paintbrush said "Don't worry!" "I will help!"

Mixing white and a little bit of black, she got a light grey that she used to paint the sky. She then experimented with various shades and painted the clouds, snowflakes, and the entire landscape in snow.

Daniel didn't know what to do when he saw the painting that evening.

He said, "This is my favorite painting." "I will name it Magical Winter."

The next day, he was so proud of his painting that he returned to school. However, other children began to laugh at him and said:

"Your painting does not have colors"

It is not true. "It is not true. My painting is vibrant, but everything is covered with snow."

He imagined what it would look like when the snow melts.

To see beyond the real world, you need imagination. Everything is possible in the realm of dreams.

Do not look at the beauty or physical attributes of people or things. Instead, seek out their inner beauty and kindness.

The Lonely Wolf

An old wolf lived in the forest's deepest depths. He didn't have any friends, he knew all of the forest animals, but they believed the wolf was a terrible creature, and no one wanted to talk with him.

Everything seemed strange one day. It was all strange. There wasn't even a squirrel or bird singing.

The wolf believed they went to bed for winter. He continued to walk by himself.

He heard laughter suddenly and was confused as to what was happening.

He looked up and was shocked at what was before him. They all gathered around the bear's home, decorated a tree, and were singing Christmas carols.

The wolf asked, "What are you celebrating?"

The bear said, "It's Christmas, come and join me, this is a time when everyone should spend quality time with their loved ones, family, and friends."

The wolf promised that he would return in a few minutes. He went into the forest to find a gift. He found nothing, no flowers or fruits, so he decided to give something to his new friends.

He made snow and added silver glitter to it. He returned to the bear's home and placed the candles on the tables. They sparkled in the dark of the night.

Everyone was happy, and the wolf always thought of his dear friends.

A Pair Of Worn Mittens

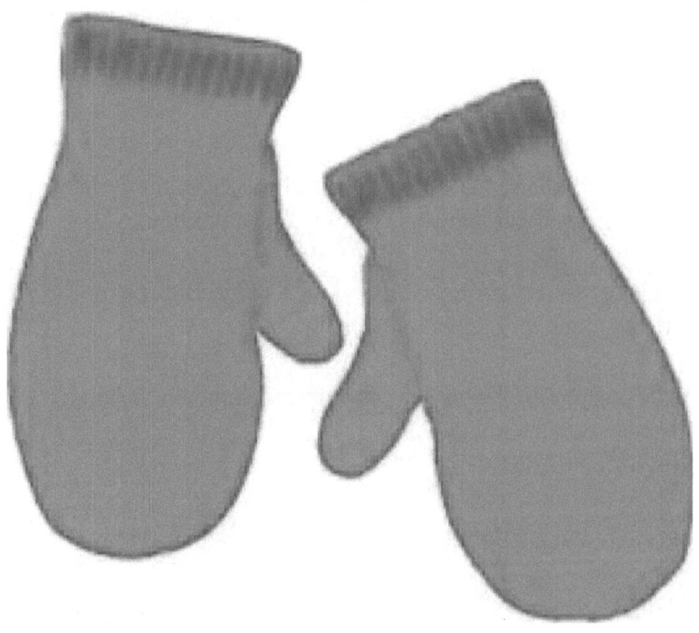

The young princess visited a candy shop in a small town near her family's castle one winter day. Everyone was stunned to see the carriage made of gold and pulled by two black horses. Although the pretty princess was able to walk around the town, it was extremely cold and her delicate hands were frozen when she arrived at the end of the evening. She didn't put on gloves.

She saw a group children playing with snowballs and laughing in front of the church.

The princess asked, "May I play?

However, when she decided to make a snowball, her hands became even more colder.

She began to weep because she had to stop playing.

Melisa, a little girl with red hair and blue eyes, was brought to the Princess by Melisa. She was a poor child who gave her an old pair red mittens.

Melisa said, "I can lend you my mittens, but they are worn. But my grandmother made them and will keep you warm!"

The beautiful princess replied, "Thank you so very much, you're so kind!"

She played with all of the children.

Before the princess left, she gave Melisa a small velvety pouch.

Her mom noticed that the sachet contained gem stones when she returned home. Melisa's family hasn't been poor since then.

If you can help someone, please do so. They may help you in the future.

The Snowman's Dinner

It was very cold. The snowman was built by the children together.

It appeared that he was a frozen guardian who watched over the village.

Children decided to make a Christmas dinner for the snowman on Christmas Eve. Each child brought something to share, so they set up a long table covered with an embroidered tablecloth. Each brought a piece turkey, another brought a pudding, and others brought candies, gingerbread, and after a while, the table was full.

The snowman looked happy and brightened their spirits.

They didn't get why the snowman wouldn't eat so they all went back to their homes for dinner. When they returned to their homes, they found that the snowman had not eaten.

The table was unaltered.

They discovered that a snowman doesn't eat food. Maybe he eats snow, and drinks melted icicles.

One child came up with the idea.

Let's give all these goodies to the children who are poor, because there will be a family that can't afford it all.

"No, I have another brilliant idea," said another child. "Our table is already set. Let's call the poor children to eat."

The place was alive and well within no time. After eating, they spent the afternoon playing in the snow.

The Lighted Carousel

The circus was established in the same town as Billy. Although they had several shows every evening, it was always full. Billy didn't realize he needed to buy his tickets
He had never been to ticket before so he went there every day in the hope that someone would invite him inside.
Children accompanied by their parents were allowed to enter and enjoyed the shows with elephants, lions, and monkeys.
Billy appeared again at the door but no one seemed to be able to see him. He went home, thinking that he would gain weight the next day. He had seen wild animals before he went to the zoo, but all he wanted was to see the blue carousel.
The same thing happened the next day. Christmas Eve was the final evening that the circus was present.
Billy returned to the circus and told the same story: children went in, had fun, and they laughed. Everyone left and Billy stayed there, staring at a carousel. He began to cry but the carousel suddenly lit up and started moving. Billy heard a voice say:
"You're a good boy, and this is your Christmas gift." It was the Spirit Of Christmas speaking.
He jumped on the carousel, and he went around and round a dozen times. He was very happy.
He went home as it was dark, and told his mom that the carousel was only lit for him. His mom laughed and said:
"Children have so many imaginations!"
Billy believed it, even though no one believed.

The Bear's Nap

All the animals in the forest were talking about winter's arrival.

They prepared food and made blankets from leaves to keep them warm. The bear was the only one who didn't have to worry.

A little black ant told the bear that he needed to be prepared for winter. The bear replied, "I don't know what you mean".

The ant said, "You must gather fruit and cereals when it is cold. During the winter everything is covered in snow, and how will you get food?"
The bear replied, "I don't believe you, I am joking",
The bear continued singing in the forest while all the other animals worked to obtain winter provisions.
The nights were growing longer and shorter, as well as the days. The arrival of winter was announced by the first snowflake falling.
All animals were allowed to go to church on Sunday morning because it was Sunday. The bear spoke after the Mass and said:
"I feel so tired this morning, I think that I will take a nap!"
He went home and covered himself in a soft, fluffy blanket before falling asleep.
He was late for rehearsals for the carols concert. Then he missed Christmas Eve and New Year's Eve.
Everyone was having a good time laughing.
"The bear is hibernating once again!"
After three months of winter cold, the snow finally melted and adorable snowdrops began to appear all over.
The bear got out of his den and set off to search for his favorite forest fruits.
"You can see that it is always sunny and pleasant weather. They are fruits.
Everywhere. The bear asked, "Why do you tell me stories about winter and snow?"
To the little ant.
The bear didn't know he was hibernating, and missed every winter. He decided that this Christmas he would stay up to celebrate Christmas.

The Frozen River

For many years, a rabbit lived in the forest. He once saw a lovely lady rabbit with white fur. He couldn't stop thinking about her beautiful eyes and long lashes since the moment he first saw them. He tried several times to cross the river but the current was too strong, and every attempt failed.

He was very sad. He wanted nothing more than to find the lovely white lady rabbit on the other bank.

The animals decorated the forest beautifully for Christmas, which was soon to come. Everyone was happy, except for the rabbit who fell in love.

It was very cold the night before Christmas and everything froze. The rabbit began to leap of joy in the morning. He looked at the frozen river, and began to dance and skate on the ice. He found the beautiful lady rabbit on the other side.

He invited her to his Christmas party in the forest, and she agreed. They have been happily married ever since.

Santa's Express

Edward was a young boy who was lazy. He woke up late at night, didn't want his homework done, didn't want clean, and was simply playing all day.

His mother didn't know how to proceed, but she had an idea. Santa called her and asked if she could have her son work for him for a while. He would soon learn how to get up every morning and create a daily schedule. Santa accepted and sent his magic message to Edward's village.

The mother said, "Look Edward, get on the train," "There, you can help Santa's Elfs and you can play and eat sweets throughout the day."

Edward did not hesitate to jump on the train and immediately got on board.

Santa's world was amazing, everything was white and you could smell ginger biscuits everywhere.

He entered the workshop. There were many elves working together to create toys.

Edward thought he could play, but first he had to wrap all the dolls in cute pink boxes for the girls. He then had to paint the wooden toys and glue the eyes on the teddy bear.

He told the other elves, "Now you can play."

Edward replied, "I'm so tired, I'd like to drink a cup of tea and go to bed",

The boy came home from Christmas and started helping his mom in the kitchen. He also cleaned his room, made a wreath and put it outside.

He was a very useful Christmas elf and helped Santa prepare presents for all children around the world every year.

Games

Game 1

How many Christmas wreaths you see? And how many candy canes?

Game 2

Find 5 differences between the two images:

Answer

Game 3

Find this things in the image below

Answer

Christmas Jokes

What did Adam say the day before Christmas? It's

Christmas, Eve!

What monkeys sing for Christmas?
-Jungle bells, jungle bells!

How do you know Santa is a man?
-No woman wears the same attire every year.

When a snowman loses weight?
-When the weather is getting warmer.

If someone claps on Christmas Eve he should be called as…
-Santapplause.

What is the favorite food of the elves?
-Elf-aghetti!

How did elves climbed up to Santa's castle?
-Using and elf-evator.

What kind of money are using the elves?
-Jingle bills!

How do you call an elf who just won the lottery?
-Welfy!

Which reindeer is very rude?
-"Rude"-olph!

How does Rudolph know when is Christmas?
-He looks at his calen-"deer"!

Christmas Tongue Twisters

Seven Santas sang silly songs.
Silly smelly snowman slips and slides. Running

Reindeer romp 'round red wreaths.

Eleven elves licked eleven little licorice lollipops. Comet

cuddles cute Christmas kittens carefully.

Santa's short suit shrunk.
Crazy kids clamor candy canes and Christmas cookies.

Eight elves eagerly ate everything.

Chilly chipper children cheerfully chant.

From The Author

Thank you for purchasing this book.

As adults we often forget the awe of learning something for the first time. For a child everything is a learning experience . The better we learn how to clearly describe something , with as few words as necessary , the faster the child will be able to visualize the scene in his or her mind.

As we get better to fleshing out this ideas and thoughts on the paper , children will become able faster to describe bigger ideas.

Ask yourself : how is it , what does it look like , is it sweet or sour , is it rough or smooth?

All of this things can be described with words , and as the words are spoken , you will stir the imagination of the child listener.

If you enjoy this book I would appreciate if you would find two second to write a great review on amazon. This will help other readers to share the good experience you had.

Best regards,

Vonburgun

dy

For more books please visit Vonburgundy's Amazon page

Piddo The
Baby Penguin
Thanksgiving Day

Piddo The Baby Penguin

Christmas Day

Disclaimer

Christmas carols

Jingle Bells

Dashing through the snow In a
one horse open sleigh O'er the
fields we go Laughing all the way
Bells on bob tails ring Making
spirits bright
What fun it is to laugh and sing A
sleighing song tonight

Oh, jingle bells, jingle bells Jingle all the
way
Oh, what fun it is to ride In a one
horse open sleigh Jingle bells,
jingle bells Jingle all the way
Oh, what fun it is to ride In a one
horse open sleigh

A day or two ago
I thought I'd take a ride And soon
Miss Fanny Bright
Was seated by my side The horse
was lean and lank Misfortune
seemed his lot We got into a drifted
bank
And then we got upset Oh, jingle

bells, jingle bells

Jingle all the way Oh, what
fun it is to ride
In a one horse open sleigh Jingle
bells, jingle bells Jingle all the
way
Oh, what fun it is to ride
In a one horse open sleigh yeah

Jingle bells, jingle bells Jingle all
the way
Oh, what fun it is to ride In a one
horse open sleigh Jingle bells,
jingle bells Jingle all the way
Oh, what fun it is to ride In a one
horse open sleigh

O Holy Night

O holy night! The stars are brightly shining, It is the
night of the dear Saviour's birth.
Long lay the world in sin and error pining. Till He
appeared and the Spirit felt its worth.
A thrill of hope the weary world rejoices, For yonder
breaks a new and glorious morn. Fall on your knees! Oh,
hear the angel voices! O night divine, the night when
Christ was born;
O night, O holy night, O night divine! O night,
O holy night, O night divine!

Led by the light of faith serenely beaming, With
glowing hearts by His cradle we stand.
O'er the world a star is sweetly gleaming,
Now come the wise men from out of the Orient land.
The King of kings lay thus lowly manger; In all our
trials born to be our friends.

He knows our need, our weakness is no stranger, Behold your King! Before him lowly bend!
Behold your King! Before him lowly bend!

Truly He taught us to love one another, His law is love and His gospel is peace.
Chains he shall break, for the slave is our brother.
And in his name all oppression shall cease.
Sweet hymns of joy in grateful chorus raise we, With all our hearts we praise His holy name.
Christ is the Lord! Then ever, ever praise we,
His power and glory ever more proclaim! His power and glory ever more proclaim!

Joy To The World

Joy to the world, the Lord is come!
Let earth receive her King; Let every heart prepare Him room,
And Heaven and nature sing, And Heaven and nature sing,
And Heaven, and Heaven, and nature sing.

Joy to the world, the Savior reigns!
Let men their songs employ;
While fields and floods, rocks, hills and plains Repeat the sounding joy,
Repeat the sounding joy, Repeat, repeat, the sounding joy.

No more let sins and sorrows grow, Nor thorns infest the ground;
He comes to make His blessings flow Far as the curse is found,

Far as the curse is found, Far as, far
as, the curse is found.

He rules the world with truth and grace, And makes
the nations prove
The glories of His righteousness, And
wonders of His love, And wonders of
His love,
And wonders, wonders, of His love.

www.ingramcontent.com/pod-product-compliance
Lightning Source LLC
LaVergne TN
LVHW041236150826
845673LV00008B/2393

* 9 7 9 8 7 5 5 4 6 0 7 2 9 *